My Name is Madie

By Jenifer Morrissey

First published in the United States in 2012
Copyright © Jenifer Morrissey, 2012

All rights reserved. No part of this publication may be reproduced, stored in a retrieval system, or transmitted in any form or by any means without the prior permission of the copyright holder.

ISBN: 978-0-578-13161-0

Published by:
Willowtrail Farm
P.O. Box 1034
Gould, Colorado, 80480 USA
in conjunction with lulu.com

Dedicated to June Langcake

*With thanks to Joe and June Langcake,
Ian and Margaret Dixon,
and Frank Long III*

For Anna

With love from Aunt Jen

Chapter 1: Who Am I?

My name is Madie. My name rhymes with 'lady,' as in 'of good breeding, of good family.' I was born on May 7, 2011 at Willowtrail Farm in the Rocky Mountains near Gould, Colorado. I am a solid black Fell Pony. My full name is Willowtrail Spring Maiden, which is pretty self-explanatory given where I was born, what time of year I was born, and my gender.

Humans have been an important part of my life for as long as I can remember. I like them, but I don't think all ponies feel that way. My mom and dad both like them, so maybe that's why I do. My mom especially enjoys being with humans. My human mum and dad are Jenifer and Don.

My human dad, Mom, and me

My parents are also Fell Ponies. My mom is Shelley and my dad is Apollo. They were born in England where most Fell Ponies live. They got to Willowtrail Farm by flying on an airplane and traveling in trucks and trailers. It took them a few weeks to make the trip. My dad left England and came to Willowtrail Farm in 2005, and my mom made the journey in 2006. They were both two when they made the trip.

My parents Shelley and Apollo

My mom's full name is Restar Mountain Shelley III. Like Willowtrail, 'Restar' refers to the farm where my mom was born. Her human mum and dad are June and Joe. June and Joe owned a farm where they bred Shorthorn cattle for dairying for many years and used Restar to name their cattle, too. Now June and Joe just raise Fell Ponies.

'Mountain' in my mom's name refers to her mother, Townend Mountain Gypsy IV. The place in England where my mom and dad's families live is very hilly, which is why 'mountain' is used in my granddam's name. My mom's name 'Shelley' comes from Joe and June's granddaughter. My mom is her mom's third daughter with the name Shelley. One of the other Shelleys lives in Germany and the other in Holland.

My human dad Don and my granddam Townend Mountain Gypsy IV. That's my mom's human dad Joe in the background.

Chapter 2: My Birth

Me at twelve hours old

The first time I saw a human was when I was born, but of course I had heard them long before that. I listened to their voices when I was inside my mom. I think they sometimes even talked to me!

The first time I touched a human was actually before I was born. My mom got very sick and had to go to a hospital. She had a terrible tummy ache. The doctor put his arm inside my mom to check for what was the matter, and he touched me while he was exploring my mom's lower digestive track. Lucky for me, the doctor made my mom feel better.

My mom chose to have me in the middle of the night. My human mum Jenifer had asked my mom to let her be at my birth. Jenifer told me that she set an alarm but it didn't go off, whatever that means, so my mom had to call out to her, silently of course, so she would come. Jenifer arrived as I was kicking my way out of the birth sack.

Mom deposited me in a very muddy spot, so Jenifer picked me up and moved me to a nice soft bed of straw. I didn't lay down long, though! All young ponies like me get up and going within fifteen minutes of being born. I had lots of energy!

My human mum did all kinds of things that first day. She touched me all over, washed my navel, and picked up all my feet. She said it was to help me do well in my life with humans. All I know is I liked the attention! I also liked making Jenifer laugh by yawning really, really big! Jenifer says both my parents and my older brother do this, too.

Mom and me when I was twelve hours old

Chapter 3: Movie Star!

Standing still for a brief moment while becoming a movie star

When I was two days old, I began exploring the pen Mom and I lived in, mostly at full speed. My human mum Jenifer set up a camera and took video of me running back and

On the move!

forth and having fun.

Actually, the video wasn't all of me running. I liked walking up to Jenifer to say hi. She said being that close made for lousy pictures. She called them nostril shots. I was just sniffing that round black shiny thing!

I must have looked pretty good running around, because then my human mum put all my short bursts of speed into a longer movie. She then published it so other people could watch. I was a movie star at two days old!

It turns out that being a movie star made a big difference in my life. A person named Frank watched it, and he instantly fell in love with me. Most people do when they meet me in person, but Frank only saw the movie. He had decided he wanted a Fell Pony, and then when he saw the movie of me, he decided I was the one for him. I'll tell you more about Frank later.

Sniffing that black shiny thing

Chapter 4: Outings

At three days old, my human mum and dad took Mom and me out of our pen for a walk. I had no idea the world was so big! I got to look at my reflection in a mud puddle, discover a rock, and run around without fences. It was fun to go FAST! After that first time, my human mum took Mom and I out every day and let us wander around. Sometimes Mom would run fast with me!

On one of my first outings

When I was four days old, I experienced my first snow storm. I was born at the end of an unusually snowy winter. Willowtrail Farm had seventy percent more snow than usual, so in May when I was born there was a lot of it still around. When I first got to venture out of the pen Mom and I shared, I got to explore it with my nose and then my feet. It's cold and wet!

My first snowstorm

On our outings, Mom wasn't nearly as impressed with the snow as I was. She wanted green grass! I guess the lingering snow covered up food that she normally eats that time of year.

Escaping insects in the shop

I didn't enjoy our outings later in the summer as much as those early days. The insects were annoying, and I just wanted to get away from them. I figured out a good place to go, though. The shop attached to the house my human parents live in is always cool in the morning, and the bugs don't like to go in there. I do!

One day while Mom and I were on an outing, a car came up to the house. The dogs that live here went to see the people as they got out, so I decided I would go, too. I think the people were surprised that a pony would be part of their greeting party!

Chapter 5: Training

When I was two days old, my human mum showed me something made of rope and rubbed me all over with it. She called it a halter. Then she started setting it over the bridge of my nose then putting another part of it around my neck. She seemed really pleased when I let her do these things. When I was five days old I even let her tie the halter on my head.

My human mum teaching me about halters and leading

When I was ten days old, my human mum started pulling on the halter when it was on my head. She seemed really pleased when I would follow her. Sometimes I even went where she wanted when she just pointed. She considered this pretty exciting!

While my human mum thinks she was training me, I was also training her. Whenever I would see her, I would call out to her. Then she would come over to say hello and often scratch me in one of my favorite places. Now I call out to her whenever I can so I get good scratches!

When I was six weeks old, I took my first ride in the horse trailer. I sure see why my mom likes to go for rides. There was lots of grass at the other end of the trip! My human dad had to help me get in the trailer the first time, but I knew what to do when it was time to come home. There were lots of bugs at pasture, so getting in the trailer was a bit of a relief, getting away from them. After a few trips, I was even getting in the trailer before my mom did!

Mom and me at pasture the first day. I worked my tail hard because of the insects.

Chapter 6: Feeding Time

While Mom and I lived in the pen where I was born, my human mum always came out first thing in the morning to give us some hay. One morning, instead of greeting my human mum at the fence like I usually did, I decided to show her my newest trick. She thought when she didn't see me that I would be sleeping in a pile of straw, but I had another use of straw in mind. In the far depths of the shed, there were bales of straw. I figured out how to stand with my front feet up on a bale. I was quite proud of myself!

Mom and me waiting to be fed.

In the middle of the day when we'd get fresh hay, I always thought it was a good time for a nap. I liked to take a few nibbles of the hay to please my mom, but then I liked to lay down in the hay. It smelled good, and my mom was always nearby eating away. When my mom eats hay, she likes to sort it. First she tosses the pile with her nose then pushes it around to get the fine bits first before working on the coarser pieces. One day my mom was especially active throwing hay around and she completely covered me up. The only thing you could see of me was my head! My hay blanket made my human mom laugh.

A modest hay blanket. Mom usually did better!

Chapter 7: The Herd

When Mom and I would go on outings, we'd see other ponies around the farm. I could see several from our pen. Once, when I was just a week old I went to say hi to a big blond pony named Torrin. After touching noses with him, I lowered my head, and suddenly I was able to walk into his paddock. But then when I wanted to leave, I ran into a fence. I didn't know fences could be a single strand of wire that you could walk under but not through. It was scary but then I was back with Mom and it was all right.

The herd watching me jealously as I eat bits of green. This is the herd I could see from the pen I shared with Mom.

My half-brother Jonty and me.

When I was a couple of months old, my human mum put Mom and me in with some other ponies. Jonty was my favorite. He's my half-brother. He was very polite to me. I was, of course, polite to him, opening my mouth and working my jaw, showing him that I am a youngster and mean him no harm.

Mostly, the herd I care about is my humans. Once, when I was at pasture with my mom, my human mum came to visit. As usual, she said hello by scratching me in my favorite places. Then she went walking off alone into our pasture. I left my mom's side and went to see what my human mum was doing. She was very happy to see me and scratched me in my favorite places again.

My human dad telling me how happy he was to see me after I scared him.

One day I guess I scared my humans. They came to pasture to see us like usual, but they could only see my mom. I could hear them, but I was taking a sunbath and didn't want to move. Then I heard them calling my name a little frantically, so I flopped my tail so they could see where I was. They were so happy to find me that I got LOTS of scratches in my favorite places while I was still lying down and after I got up!

Chapter 8: Leaving Willowtrail Farm

One day in the fall, my human mum came out in the evening and spent time with me. It was unusual since she didn't usually visit me that time of day. She scratched me in all my favorite places and told me how special I am. For some reason, she had tears streaming from her eyes. I stayed close to her as long as she wanted me to.

The next morning my human mum fed me especially early in the morning. Then I heard a truck and trailer pull into the farm before the sun was even up. My human mum came to get me like she usually does to lead me down to be with the herd, but this time we passed that gate and went towards the strange truck and trailer.

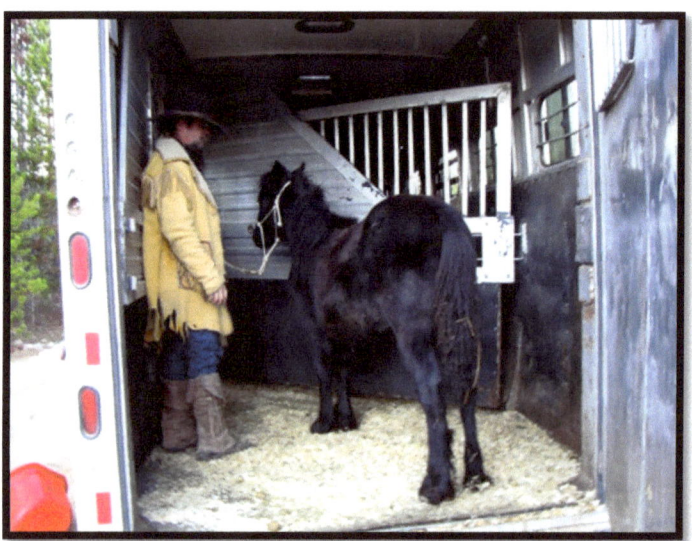

Leaving Willowtrail Farm in a strange trailer

I got into the trailer like I always do, even though it was different. There were shavings on the floor, and it was bigger, but getting in is what the humans wanted, and we began a long trip.

Chapter 9: My New Home

When my long trip ended, I was greeted by a very happy human named Frank. He's my number one human now. We live on a five acre farm in Tennessee with dogs and goats and chickens. There's also a big horse named Reba.

Reba and me on a frosty morning

When I first met Reba, I thought I could boss her around. One day I even chased her all over the pasture. Now I just let her think she's boss. The one I really care about is Frank, and when I see him, I run to him. He seems to like that. Then I follow him around the pasture when he comes out to see me, unless there's a particularly choice morsel I just have to eat. As soon as it's in my mouth, though, I trot to keep up with him.

I get along well with the other farm animals. One day a rooster landed on my back. I just pushed him off with my nose. Another day there was a little goat that was hurt and couldn't stand up. I took a mouthful of hay and dropped it in front of him so he could eat.

One day my human was cleaning out the tank where we drink water. When he dumped out the old water, there was a green thing in it that jumped. I went up to it and sniffed it, and it jumped again. So I sniffed it again, and it jumped again. Then I sniffed it again, and it jumped again. This was fun, so I kept doing it. Then I changed the game and put my foot on it. But then when I sniffed it, it didn't jump. I looked at my human Frank because I didn't understand why the jumping thing didn't play the game anymore. My human couldn't stop laughing.

Frank giving me a hug when I arrived at his farm in the middle of the night

There are lots of insects here at my new home. My human thought he could help me keep them away from my face by putting something called a fly mask on my head. I ran around and around the field trying to get rid of it then went to the water trough and tried to wash it off. I finally figured out how to take it off so I can see again.

One of the goats had a baby. I was there when it was born. I learn so much by smelling. I smelled the baby then I smelled the mom's back end. I guess the baby came out of there. Whenever the baby cries, I go to say hello to it.

When the baby goat was a few days old, I heard it crying like it was hungry. It was in the barn, and its mom was in the pasture, so I went out to the pasture and herded the mom into the barn so the baby could get some milk. I kept that mom there until the baby had enough to eat. Then the baby went out to the pasture near the fence along the road. Suddenly some people came along the road riding horses. I ran at the fence and whinnied at the horses to keep them away from my baby goat.

Chapter 10: My Human Frank

Sometimes my human Frank goes away for several days to do things with dogs. I guess he makes them look pretty and fancy so they get ribbons and awards. I like it better when he's home. When I hear him come home, I run to the fence whinnying a greeting.

Frank and me

One night I had to protect him. Coyotes were singing really loudly at the bottom of the pasture, and it must have upset my human because he came running out of the house into the pasture waving a big knife. He ran towards the coyotes, and I didn't like that so I ran to him whinnying as loud as I could. Then I ran between him and the coyotes and tried to herd him back to the barn. When he tried to go around me, I wrapped my body around him to prevent him from going further. I was only six months old when this happened and I'd only lived with Frank for a month, but I already cared about him and wanted to protect him.

Chapter 11: My Name is Madie

My mom's human mom June has been quite sick recently. My human mum Jenifer is good friends with my mom's human parents, so Jenifer's been quite concerned about June. My dad's human parents, Ian and Margaret, are also good friends with June and Joe. They've also been quite concerned about June. And of course Joe and June's children, including their son Joseph, have been concerned about June.

Joseph, Jenifer, and Ian and Margaret found ways to help June. She's now feeling much better, which makes Joe happy, too. It's good to have good humans and for them to be happy.

My name is Madie

My name is Madie, which rhymes with lady. I think I come from good breeding and good family. My human mum Jenifer told me many times that I am special. My human Frank says that I make his life complete. Whatever those things mean, I know that I like my people, and they like me.

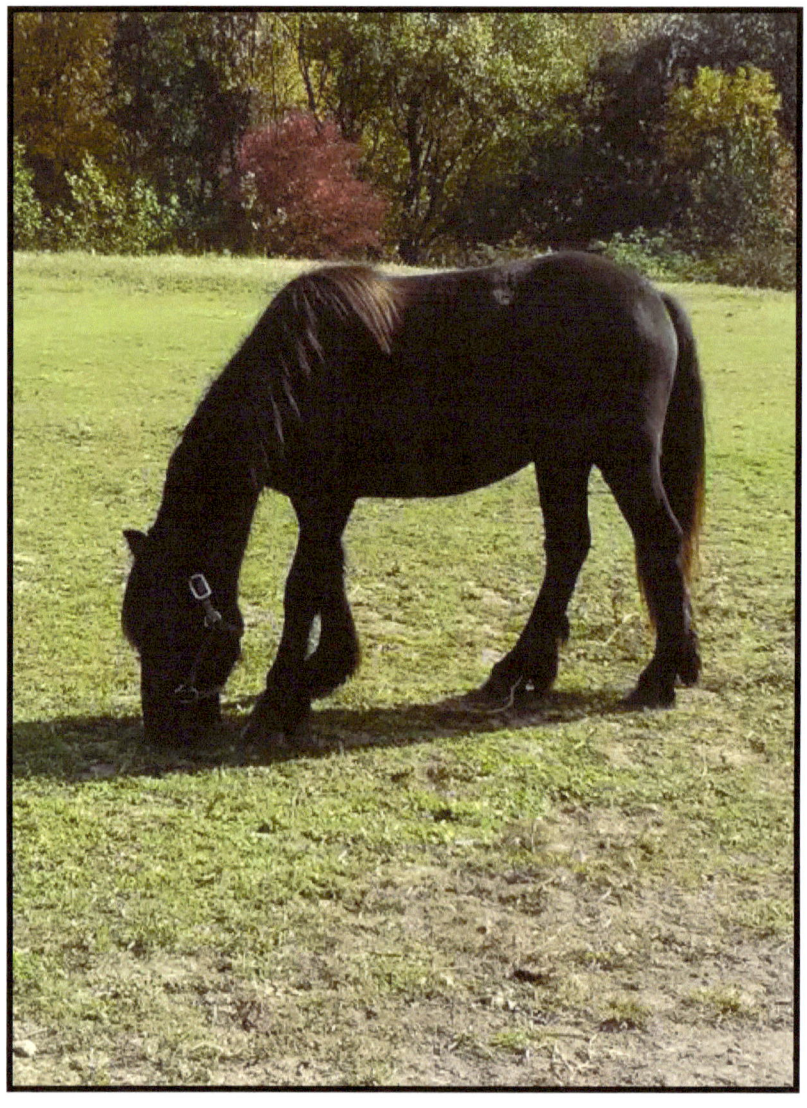

My name rhymes with lady: of good breeding and good family.

Postscript

June Langcake passed away the 12th of June, 2013. She spent the final months of her life free of asthma symptoms, with which she had lived for over seventy years, and free from the symptoms of cancer with which she had been diagnosed a year previously. She continued to be interested in the ponies that she and Joe bred until her last day.

About the Author

Jenifer Morrissey has owned and bred Fell Ponies since 2000. She has a bachelors degree in electrical engineering from Stanford University and a masters in environmental policy and management from the University of Denver. She raises rare breeds of livestock and owns a logging business with her husband in Gould, Colorado. Jenifer is the author of *A Humbling Experience: My First Few Years with Fell Ponies*, published in 2009.

www.ingramcontent.com/pod-product-compliance
Lightning Source LLC
Chambersburg PA
CBHW041807160426
43202CB00001B/8